THE GREAT PYRAMID OF CHEOPS

by Steven Thomsen

PUBLISHED BY

Capstone Press

Mankato, MN, U.S.A.

Distributed By

ⓅⓅ CHILDRENS PRESS ®
CHICAGO

CIP

LIBRARY OF CONGRESS CATALOGING IN PUBLICATION DATA

Thomsen, Steven.
The Great Pyramid of Cheops / by Steven Thomsen
p. cm.--(Inside story)
Summary: Describes ancient Egyptian civilization and the
construction and uses of the pyramids, with emphasis on the
Pyramid of Cheops.
ISBN 1-56065-024-9
1. Great Pyramid (Egypt)--Juvenile literature. [1. Pyramids--Egypt.
2. Egypt--Antiquities.] I. Title II. Series. III. Series: Inside story
(Mankato, Minn.)
DT63.T46 1989   932--dc20   **89-25179 CIP AC**

PHOTO CREDITS

Art Resource: 4, 19, 43
Egyptian Tourist Authority: 11, 13, 40

Designed by Nathan Y. Jarvis & Associates, Inc.

Capstone Press

Box 669, Mankato, MN, U.S.A. 56001

CONTENTS

INTRODUCTION

Oliver gazed up at the tall columns at the entrance of the British Museum. Oliver liked to come to London and visit his Aunt Bess. Today she was taking him to see Ginger.

Back home in New York, Oliver also liked to spend Saturdays visiting museums. He especially liked to see ancient **artifacts** from Egypt. Today was going to be very special.

"Aunt Bess," Oliver asked, "who is Ginger?"

"Why, Ginger is a famous mummy," Aunt Bess explained as they reached the top of the steps and entered the museum.

"A scary one, like in old movies?" Oliver wondered.

"Oh, no, not like that," Aunt Bess said

with a smile. "Ginger is a 5,000-year-old Egyptian mummy that is on display here at the museum. We're going to see him today."

"Wow! A real mummy!" Oliver said. "How did he get his name?"

"He was named Ginger because of the reddish, ginger-colored locks of hair that are still on his head," Oliver's aunt explained. "The Egyptians would use salt to dry out their dead and then wrap them tightly with cloth into mummies. The mummies would then be buried inside great pyramids or special tombs. Because the climate in Egypt is so dry, the mummies were preserved," she said.

"Have you ever seen a real pyramid?" Oliver asked.

"Why, yes," Aunt Bess explained. "When I was about your age, Grandpa Hank took me to Egypt to see the Pyramids of Giza. They are magnificent!"

"We're learning about pyramids in school," Oliver said.

Suddenly, Oliver and Aunt Bess saw the mummy exhibit. "Oh, boy!" Oliver shouted. He hurried over for a closer look.

EGYPT: LAND OF THE GREAT PYRAMIDS

When you think of Egypt, you probably think of camels, deserts, and of course, pyramids. But did you know that Egypt is also called the birthplace of western civilization? Egypt is about the same size as Texas. About 34 million people live there today. It is located in the northeast corner of Africa.

Much of what we know about ancient history we have learned from studying Egypt and the pyramids. The Pyramids of Giza are very famous. They are more than 4,500 years old. The pyramids tell us a great deal about people who lived a long time ago.

The ancient Egyptians built about 80 pyramids in the Giza Valley. Giza is near

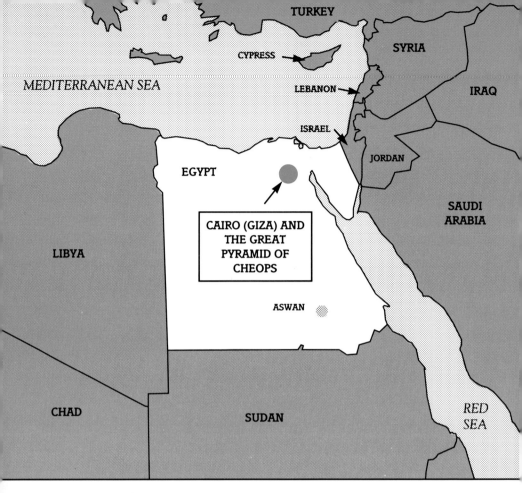

Egypt, Giza and the location of the Great Pyramid.

Cairo, which is the capital of Egypt. Sometimes Giza is spelled "Gizeh."

Of all the great Pyramids of Giza, the biggest, and most famous, is the Pyramid of Cheops. It was built to be a tomb for King Khufu. Khufu was Cheops' Egyptian name.

He ruled Egypt around 2500 B.C. It took more than 20 years to build the Pyramid of Cheops. It took 10 years just to build a road to reach it. The Pyramid of Cheops also is called the Great Pyramid. It is one of the Seven Wonders of the Ancient World.

Next to the Pyramid of Cheops, two other kings also built pyramids. These pyramids were used as their tombs. These kings were named Khafre and Menkure. Khafre was Cheops' brother. Menkure was his nephew. Khafre's pyramid looks bigger than Cheops'. That is because it was built on higher ground. It is actually smaller. These three pyramids are famous because they are three of the biggest in all of Egypt.

To understand the pyramids and why they were built, you must understand something about the people of ancient Egypt.

ANCIENT EGYPT AND ITS PEOPLE

The first people came to Egypt as early as 5000 B.C. That was almost 7,000 years ago. Egypt is a hot, sunny desert region. People came to Egypt because of the Nile River, the world's longest river. The Nile River runs through the middle of Egypt for nearly 930 miles. It flows northward and winds through the country. It finally empties into the Mediterranean Sea.

About a half a mile wide, the Nile River has created a fertile valley of land where flowers and trees grow and where crops can be planted. On both sides of this green, lush river valley, however, stretch two great deserts. As the river fans out into the sea it creates a broad **delta**. A delta is a deposit of rich soil and silt. Silt is made of fine bits of rock and soil that are washed along by the river.

The first people to live along the banks of the Nile River valley probably built reed huts and lived in small groups. They used the rich clay along the river to make pottery jars and utensils for cooking.

During the next 800 years or so they gradually formed larger groups and learned to work together. They made copper tools and mud bricks. They became better farmers. They learned to trade with other groups of

A view of the Nile River.

people. They raised sheep, goats, cattle and donkeys. They even made sailboats and traveled up and down the Nile River.

The ancient Egyptians learned to live with an event of nature called the **annual inundation**. This was the period from July through November when the Nile River would flood. The flood waters would cover the farm lands. But this was actually good.

Each year when the flood waters receded, a new layer of rich earth was left behind. This was a blessing for Egyptian farms. Today, the Aswan High Dam at the tip of Lake Nasser has ended the annual inundation.

The ancient Egyptians had a language of their own, of course. They even developed a method to write their language. Their written language became known as **hieroglyphics**, or "sacred writings." This is because the writings often appeared in religious temples. They were considered the "words of the gods." Hieroglyphics used pictures and shapes to tell stories and tell of important events. Hieroglyphics also were painted on buildings, both inside and out. **Archeologists**, people who study ancient civilization, have learned to read these messages. The messages tell us what Egyptian life was like.

Hieroglyphics were painted on many buildings and temples, often telling stories of gods and pharaohs.

About 3100 B.C., Egypt united and became one great and powerful nation. Its first great king was King Menes. Cheops, or Khufu as he was called by the Egyptians, became king about 600 years later. At that time, Egypt was in a period that historians call the "Fourth Dynasty." It was during this period that many pyramids were built. The Great Pyramid of Cheops was built during this time. The people who lived in Giza and Memphis at that time called it "Aknet Khufu." Translated, "Aknet Khufu" means the "Splendor of Khufu" or "Khufu in the Horizon."

In Egypt, the kings were the center of attention in all activities. Egyptian kings were called **pharaohs**. The Egyptians thought of their pharaohs as having great and special powers. The people worshipped the pharaoh as a god. The pharaohs commanded and led the armies. They made decisions on how Egypt would deal with neighboring countries. They even settled arguments that could not be dealt with in court. Pharaohs also traveled to visit and inspect other settlements in the kingdom. They gave permission to build temples and pyramids. And they led important social and religious ceremonies.

For Cheops, nothing was of more interest or importance than building pyramids. His father, Seneferu, had been the first pharaoh to build a true pyramid. In fact, Seneferu built three pyramids. His first pyramid was built in Meidum, a city 30 miles from Memphis. But this pyramid was never used. The second pyramid he built is the famous "Bent Pyramid." It is in Dahshur. This began as a normal-looking pyramid. But half way to the top, the angle becomes much steeper. It actually looks like a small pyramid was built on top of a larger one.

His third pyramid was also built at Dahshur. It was a very large pyramid. The writings on it say that it was built in only three years. This pyramid may have given Cheops the idea to build his own.

Cheops wanted his pyramid to be the biggest and most perfect that had ever been built.

HOW THE PYRAMID GOT ITS NAME

The Egyptian word for pyramid was "mr" or "mer." To describe the height of a pyramid, the Egyptians used the words "per-em-us." But it may have been the Greeks that turned the words "per-em-us" into the word "pyramis." Some people disagree, though. The Greeks also used the word "pyramis" to describe a "wheaten cake." The cakes, when baked, were shaped much like the pyramids.

Some people who call themselves "**mystics**" say the word "pyramid" may have had an even more mysterious origin. These people believe that "Pyr" is the ancient Egyptian name for Cheops. "Pyr" may secretly mean "The Light" and refer to the Zodiac. Either way, the Greek word "pyramis" has become the modern word "pyramid."

MUMMIES AND EGYPTIAN RELIGIOUS BELIEFS

The Egyptians liked to have fun. They liked funny stories. They liked to be entertained by musicians and acrobats. Many children had monkeys for pets. The Egyptians also were very religious people. The Egyptians worshipped many different gods. One of the most popular gods was Ra, the sun god. Hathor was their goddess of love. The Egyptians used a cow to represent her in their hieroglyphics. Thoth was the god of wisdom. He was drawn as a baboon with a dog's head.

Two other important gods were Osiris and his wife, Isis. The Egyptians believed that Osiris was killed by his jealous brother, Seth. Seth was jealous because of Osiris' success at growing plants and crops. His brother then scattered parts of his body in the Nile. Isis gathered his parts. She prayed to the sun god who sent **Anubis** to help. Anubis put the body back together. He wrapped it in bandages and held a proper funeral. The legend says that Isis then fanned the body with her wings and Osiris came back to life.

The story of Osiris was important to the ancient Egyptians. They also believed in life after death. Egyptians preserved the bodies of people who died by wrapping them into mummy form. They did this the same way that Anubis wrapped Osiris. By doing this, they believed the dead person's soul would continue to exist.

Actually, they believed that more than one soul for each person would continue to exist. One soul was called the **ba**. The Egyptians believed that the ba continued to live on earth and returned to the body at night. The **ka** was the person's spiritual duplicate. The Egyptians believed that the ka traveled between the earth and a spiritual world. For the person to have eternal life, the ka and the ba had to be able to identify the body. The Egyptians used **mummification** to make this possible.

It took about 70 days for the Egyptians to finish making a mummy. Once the mummy

A scene from the tomb of King Tut.

was ready, it was buried with some of the dead
person's favorite things. These were things
such as pottery, clothes, furniture and jewelry.

The Egyptians thought the dead might need their favorite possessions in the next life. Because the climate is dry in Egypt, mummies and their belongings have survived for thousands of years inside the pyramids and special tombs.

In the very early days of Egypt, long before the pharaohs, the dead were simply buried in graves dug in the sand. In the early days of the first kings, brick shelters were built over the graves. These were called **mastabas**. The shelters were about eight feet high. They were built by kings and wealthy people. Each king tried to build the biggest and most elaborate mastabas. These mastabas became bigger and fancier.

By the time Cheops was the pharaoh, the mastabas had grown so large that they had become pyramids. The man who made the first pyramid from a mastaba was Imhotep. Imhotep was an architect who worked for Pharaoh Zoser. When Imhotep first built Zoser's burial place, the mastaba was 26 feet high. Each side was 200 feet long. He kept building and adding to it. Eventually it reached 200 feet high. The sides were 400 feet by 350 feet. Imhotep finished it by covering it with limestone blocks. It looked like several giant steps. Many other "step" pyramids were built after that. All pyramids were built with smooth sloping sides after about 200 years.

Imhotep became an Egyptian legend. Later, the Egyptians worshipped him as a god of learning and medicine. He had become very popular.

HERODOTUS, THE GREAT PYRAMID EXPLORER

Oliver looked closely inside the mummy cases. He was fascinated by the colorful shapes and images of the hieroglyphics painted inside. "Someday, I'd like to visit the pyramids, too," he told his aunt.

"There have been many famous explorers," Aunt Bess explained. "One of the very first was Herodotus."

"Who was he?" Oliver asked.

"Herodotus visited the Pyramids of Giza more than 2,400 years ago. He wrote a book about it. You see, the pyramids were already very old when he first saw them," Aunt Bess said.

Oliver listened carefully as his aunt told him the story of Herodotus.

About 2,100 years after Cheops built his pyramid, it was visited by Herodotus of Halicarnassus. Herodotus was born in 484 B.C. in the Greek colony of Halicarnassus. Halicarnassus was in Asia Minor. Today Asia Minor is the country we know as Turkey.

Herodotus died in 426 B.C. He spent the last 17 years of his life traveling across the land and the seas. He saw many famous places and things. He visited Athens and the islands of the Aegean Sea. He even went to a place north of the Black Sea. When he visited the area it was called Scythia. It was a dangerous place to visit because only barbarians lived there then. Today it is a peaceful place. It is now part of the Soviet Union.

On one of his trips, Herodotus sailed up the Nile River. When he arrived in Giza he visited the Pyramid of Cheops. On his many trips, Herodotus wrote about the things he had seen and visited. Eventually, he wrote an entire book. His book was filled with exciting and interesting stories. His book tells us many things about the pyramids and the Pyramid of Giza. In fact, many of the things that we know about the history of the pyramids we learned from his book. In his writing, Herodotus used the Greek names for kings who built the pyramids. Cheops is Greek for Khufu. And in Greek, Khafre's name was Chepren and Menkure's name was Mycerinus.

If you were to visit the pyramids today you could hire a guide to give you a tour. This is also what Herodotus did. He hired Egyptian guides who told him about the great legends of the pyramids. They also told him many facts about the Pyramid of Cheops and how it was built.

FUN FACTS ABOUT THE PYRAMID OF CHEOPS

"How big are the pyramids?" Oliver asked his aunt. "What did Herodotus find inside? How many men did it take to build Cheops' pyramid?"

"Slow down Oliver. You've got so many questions. Let's answer them one at a time," Aunt Bess said. Oliver continued to listen as his aunt told him more about Herodotus' visit to the pyramids.

Like Oliver, Herodotus had many questions about the pyramids. His Egyptian guides told him what life was like for Cheops' people. They told him that Cheops forced thousands of men to work very hard to build his pyramid. There were not enough men in

Giza to build his pyramid. So Cheops brought in men from other cities to work. As many as 100,000 people may have worked on the pyramid at one time. About every three months, Cheops brought in new workers.

Each of the four sides of the Pyramid of Cheops is about 756 feet wide at its base. The sides slant gracefully upward until they form a point. The tip of the point is about 450 feet high. The Egyptian guides told Herodotus that the pyramid was 800 feet high. This could not have been possible. However, the pyramid once was about 30 feet higher. But in about 650 A.D., a band of invading Arabs stole the stones on top and used them to build their own buildings.

The smallest stones used to build the Pyramid of Cheops were at least 30 feet wide. Many of these enormous stones had to be dragged from the quarries in the Arabian Hills. They were transported along the Nile River. Others came from the Libyan Hills. Many of the stones were floated in flat-bottomed boats down the Nile.

As many as 2,300,000 stones were used to build the Pyramid of Cheops. The lightest stones were not all that light. They weighed at least 2 1/2 tons. The heaviest blocks averaged about 15 tons. In fact, all the stones in the pyramid together weigh about 6 million tons. That's more than 20 times the weight of New York's Empire State Building.

If you laid the stones side by side, they would stretch at least two-thirds of the way around the world. When Napolean visited the Pyramids of Giza in 1798 he thought there would be enough stones to build a tall wall all the way around France.

THE BUILDING OF THE GREAT PYRAMID OF GIZA

"How did they get such large stones up so high?" Oliver asked.

"Herodotus said the pyramid was built with machines," Aunt Bess explained. "If the Egyptians had machines, they were nothing like the large cranes and equipment used to build our skyscrapers today."

Oliver tried to imagine what life would have been like on an Egyptian work crew. "I'll bet it was fun," he said.

"Well, Oliver, I'm not sure the Egyptians thought it was fun," Aunt Bess said. "But Cheops may not have been the tyrant that Herodotus wrote about. They worshipped their king and were willing to work for Cheops."

"Did they get rich with all that work?" Oliver asked.

"The guides told Herodotus that the workers were paid in food and clothing," his aunt explained.

"Food?" Oliver asked.

"According to the guides, horseradishes, garlic and onions were very popular," Aunt Bess said.

Oliver shook his head and wrinkled his nose at the thought of a supper of onions and horseradishes.

Building the Pyramid of Cheops was no small task. It took many different people with many different skills. There were stone cutters, surveyors, masons, foremen, mortar makers and carpenters. An important worker was the architect, the person who designed the pyramid and its inside chambers. The Pyramid of Cheops may have had many architects. Archeologists believe this because of the many chambers inside and the various styles of workmanship. There are at least three main chambers. This is because Cheops may have kept changing his mind about where in the pyramid he wanted to be buried.

People have written of "secret" Egyptian methods for building pyramids. There have been stories of lost secrets for moving and placing the stones. However, we have learned much of how the pyramids may have been built. The hieroglyphics and paintings inside tombs and temples have revealed many of the "secrets." A famous painting can still be seen on the wall of the tomb of an Egyptian nobleman. It was painted about 800 years after the Pyramid of Cheops was built. It shows 172 men pulling a large stone statue on a sled. It shows water, or another liquid, being poured on the ground in front of the path of the sled. This was to reduce friction and to make the sled easier to pull.

The "machines" that Herodotus wrote about were probably wooden planks. These planks, along with crowbars, sleds, and wooden rollers, enabled the work teams to raise and position the heavy stone blocks. Each stone may have been rocked and tipped sideways with the crowbars. A wooden sled could be placed under it. The workers would have then tied the stone to the sled with strong rope. Next, the sled would have been propped up by crowbars. Round logs may have been slipped underneath. The logs were used as rollers. This made it much simpler to roll the heavy stone blocks from the quarries to the flat-bottomed boats to the construction site. About eight men worked on each block at a time.

The Pyramid of Cheops was built on a small hill on the west bank of the Nile River. First, the area for the base of the pyramid was cleared. The original burial chamber was cut out of the rock below the surface of the sandy ground. Plans provided for a long, narrow hallway to slope down into this chamber. Today, it is known as the Descending Corridor. The entrance actually begins 55 feet above the ground on the north side of the pyramid. It is only 4 feet high and 3 1/2 feet wide. The corridor stretches for more than several hundred feet through the pyramid and into the rock below the base. The underground chamber, which was never used as Cheops' burial room, is 46 feet long, 27 feet wide and 11 feet high.

When the underground chamber was complete, all the blocks that formed the pyramid's base were set in place. The builders now faced a new challenge. The massive stone blocks now had to be lifted to higher and higher levels. To make this possible, four new work crews were brought in. Each crew built sloping ramps of dirt along each side of the pyramid. These ramps could not be too steep.

The ramps were used to drag and pull the blocks on sleds up to each level. As the pyramid neared completion it was almost covered with dirt ramps.

At the tip of the pyramid the builders placed a large, pointed **capstone**, the final block. Now, the builders began to work back down the pyramid. An **outer casing** of white limestone was added to the pyramid. These last blocks were cut, finished and placed with great care. They gave the pyramid a smooth, shiny surface. As the builders moved downward, the dirt ramps were taken away. Finally, the Great Pyramid stood finished, glistening in the sun.

When Herodotus visited the pyramid it must have been an impressive sight. He made notes on the precision and skill of the builders. He saw how careful the builders were. Great attention was paid to each detail. The Egyptian builders had cut and placed the large stones so carefully that most were separated by no more than 1/50th of an inch. The pyramid's four sides were built to face true north, south, east and west. Each corner of the pyramid is nearly a perfect right angle. If Herodotus didn't notice these things, his guides certainly must have told him.

INSIDE THE GREAT PYRAMID

"No one really knows why Cheops changed his mind about being buried in the underground chamber," Aunt Bess explained.

"Maybe he thought all those big stones would smash him," Oliver suggested. He tried to imagine what it would be like buried inside a huge pyramid. "I guess it might be scary."

"Cheops had two other chambers built inside. It was unusual to be buried high up within the pyramid," Oliver's aunt said. "But he was the pharaoh. If that's what he wanted, that's the way it would be."

When Cheops changed his mind, the workers had to begin cutting through massive stones that already had been put in place. A new hallway was created. It is called the

Ascending Corridor. It actually begins in the roof of the Descending Corridor and extends up into the center of the pyramid. The entrance was hidden behind a slab of limestone that looked like the rest of the roof. This corridor leads to a second room, called the Queen's Chamber. It is located within the pyramid just above ground level.

The Queen's Chamber is a large room that measures 18 feet by 17 feet. The ceiling reaches up to a point that is 20 feet high. A close examination of the room shows that it was not part of the original plans. The architects must have allowed for it as the pyramid was being built. However, before the chamber was finished, Cheops again changed his mind.

The work crews went back to their chisels and returned to the Ascending Corridor. They tunneled upward again. Eventually, they created a beautiful passageway called the Grand Gallery. It is 28 feet high. It stretches inside the pyramid for 153 feet. Under the new plans, the Grand Gallery led to the King's Chamber. It is here, in the heart of the pyramid, that Cheops was buried. His room was majestic. The walls, which were 19 feet high, were made of granite. The room was

34 feet by 17 feet. The massive roof weighs at least 400 tons. Three other small chambers were built to help hold up the roof. Before this room was finished, a heavy black granite coffin, or **sarcophagus**, was lowered into place.

Just as you lock the door to your house at night, the Egyptians tried to "lock" the "doors" to the chambers in the pyramid. Cheops was buried with jewels, valuable treasures and many fine things. His family and friends wanted to make sure that no one could steal them from his tomb.

Three huge stone blocks were left by the last workers to block the entrance to the tomb in the King's Chamber. When the funeral was over, the blocks, or **portcullises**, were put in place. As the last people left the King's Chamber, three large blocks of granite were sent tumbling into the Ascending Corridor. This blocked the passage way. These last people in the pyramid left through a secret shaft. The final shaft and the Descending Corridor were also plugged with large stones. The Egyptians hoped that the mummy of Cheops and his possessions would be safe.

Explorers have found other small, rectangular shafts that extend away from the

King's Chamber. These may have been for ventilation. This may have been an ancient form of air conditioning. Some of the people who studied pyramids thought these shafts may have allowed some of the king's servants to be sealed inside with the king's mummy. One man who thought this was Benoit de Maillet. He was a Frenchman who visited in Egypt more than 200 years ago. Maillet thought that one of the shafts was used to slip food inside to the servants.

Herodotus' guides told him that Cheops may have even had "running water." They said that Cheops built an underground canal from the Nile River. It ran underneath the pyramid. The original tomb may have been an island in the middle of the underground canal.

RAIDERS OF THE GREAT PYRAMID

The mummy of Cheops and his many treasures may have been safe for only about 400 years. Unfortunately, many thieves eventually broke into the burial chamber. The robbers removed the stones at the entrance and found other passageways into the King's Chambers. The entrance was resealed. But others managed to break in.

One of the most famous robbers of the Pyramid of Cheops was Caliph Ma'mum. He was the son of Harun al-Rahid, a famous Arabian raider. In 818 A.D., Ma'mum took his band of men to the Pyramid of Cheops. He did not know that the mummy of Cheops and the treasures had already been taken.

Ma'mum ordered his men to break into the pyramid. They began on the pyramid's north side. They used fire and vinegar to help break the massive stones. After chiseling, cutting, and tunneling their way in, they found the King's Chamber. When they got there, the coffin and the chamber were empty. They had already been empty for thousands of years.

This made Ma'mum very angry. He decided to destroy as much of the pyramid as possible. He and his men carried away many of the limestone blocks from the outer casing. They took many blocks from the top of the pyramid. They used these stones to construct their own buildings.

After Ma'mum and his men left, others came and stole from the Great Pyramid. Eventually, all of the beautiful, polished limestone was stripped away.

REDISCOVERING THE GREAT PYRAMID

For a long time, many things about ancient Egypt and the pyramids were still a great mystery. In 1798, Napolean Bonaparte and his army sailed to Egypt. In addition to soldiers, Napolean brought along several scholars and scientists.

They visited the pyramids and measured the Sphinx. Standing almost 70 feet high, the Sphinx is cut from a large rock near Khafre's pyramid. The Sphinx has the head of a man and the body of a lion. It is about 240 feet long. Each paw is 50 feet long. It wears a royal headdress. The face is that of Khafre, who had his servants carve the Sphinx.

A year after Napolean and his army

arrived in Giza, a great discovery was made. One of Napolean's officers was digging in the mud near the mouth of the Nile. Suddenly, he struck a very hard, black stone. On the shiny surface were strange carvings that appeared to be three different languages. One of the languages was Greek. Another was Egyptian hieroglyphics. Jean Francois Champollion, a French scholar, finally translated the hieroglyphics in 1822.

This great discovery, now called the

The Sphinx in Giza.

Rosetta Stone, has unlocked the mysteries of the Egyptians and pyramids. It has made it possible to read the pictures and symbols that remain in tombs and on temple walls.

In 1954 an archeologist named Kamal al Mallakh made a new discovery. About 60 feet from the south wall of the Pyramid of Cheops he found two large, unopened chambers. Each chamber, or pit, was about 102 feet long, 8 1/2 feet wide, and 11 1/2 feet deep. Large limestone slabs covered the stone chambers. Inside one of the chambers he found the remains of a 143 foot long boat. It may have been used to float the great King's body down the river during his funeral. Kamal al Mallakh and other archeologists reassembled the ship. It is now on display in a museum built directly over the site. He never looked inside the other chamber.

In November of 1987, archeologists returned to the site. They came back to look inside the second chamber. They thought that the chamber might have been sealed so tight that it would still contain air that was thousands of years old. When Kamal al Mallakh opened the other chamber he said he could smell the "vapors, perfumes of the wood, sacred wood of the ancient religion." The archeologists wanted to be very careful as they examined the second chamber. They hoped the old air could teach them something about Egypt's climate 4,600 years ago when the chamber was sealed. They used a "space-age" drill to bore into the chamber. The drill was sealed tightly and surrounded by a vacuum chamber. The vacuum would prevent new air from entering the stone pit. It would also let them examine the old air. A miniature television camera was lowered through the hole.

Inside they saw the timbers of another ancient funeral boat. But this chamber had not remained sealed. This time, the air only smelled stale. The archeologists decided not to remove the timbers and parts of the boat from the chamber. Instead, they carefully plugged the hole they had drilled through the limestone rock.

"Wow! I never knew there were so many great stories about mummies and pyramids and stuff!" Oliver said.

"Oh, yes. And there are many more stories about ancient Egypt and great pharaohs such as King Tut. He was just a boy of only 9 when he became king. He ruled for only 10 years and died when he was 19. In his burial

The sarcophagus of King Tut.

tomb archeologists found perfumes, a golden throne and many treasures. He was buried in a solid-gold coffin that weighed 2,500 pounds!

"There is so much to tell. But we'll have to save those stories for another time," Aunt Bess explained.

Oliver took one last look at Ginger and

waved good-bye. He thought about the marvelous things he had seen. He thought about the stories his aunt had told him.

In his mind, he could see the pyramids. He thought he could hear the large, wooden sleds being dragged and pulled up the ramps. He heard the chisels and hammers. He even thought he could smell the onions and garlic for supper.

"Someday," he told his aunt. "I'm going to Egypt to see the treasures for myself."

GLOSSARY

ANNUAL INUNDATION — The period between July and November when the Nile River would flood the area in the river valley.

ANUBIS — Egyptian god with the head of a jackal who led the dead to judgement.

ARCHEOLOGIST — A person who studies prehistoric people, their dwellings, and their artifacts.

ARTIFACT — Any object made by human work.

45

BA — A person's soul. The Egyptians believed a person's ba continued to live on earth after death. At the night, the ba rests within the dead person's body.

CAPSTONE — A pointed, pyramid-shaped stone placed at the top of a pyramid.

DELTA — A fan-like deposit of rich silt and soil where the Nile River empties into the Mediterranean Sea.

HIEROGLYPHICS — It means "sacred writings." The written language of the ancient Egyptians. It used pictures and symbols.

KA — A dead person's spiritual duplicate. The Egyptians believed it traveled to and from the land of the living and the spirit world.

MASTABA — A tomb structure with sloping walls. It contained several rooms for religious offerings and the belongings of the deceased. It was built over the grave of the dead person.

MYSTIC — A person who believes he knows things that are beyond human understanding.

MUMMIFICATION — The process of preserving a dead body. It involved removing vital organs and wrapping the person in linen.

OUTER CASING — The polished limestone blocks placed on the outside of the pyramid. The outer casing gave the pyramid a smooth, shiny appearance.

PHARAOH — An Egyptian king.

PORTCULLISES — A name for the granite slabs used to seal the entrance to the pharaoh's burial chamber after the ceremony.

ROSETTA STONE — The large black stone discovered by Napolean's army. On it was carved three languages. One of the languages was actually Egyptian heiroglyphics. It made possible the translation of Egyptian heiroglyphics.

SARCOPHAGUS — The large stone outer-coffin in which the wooden coffin containing the mummy was placed.